30 Small Collages

Richard Leach

ISBN: 978-1-387-78278-9

This book presents 30 collages made on playing cards or playing card size cardboard (2.5 x 3.5 inches) between November, 2016 and July, 2017. They are reproduced here larger than life size. The media include ink, pencil, and glued paper.

richardleach.deviantart.com

lulu.com/rleach

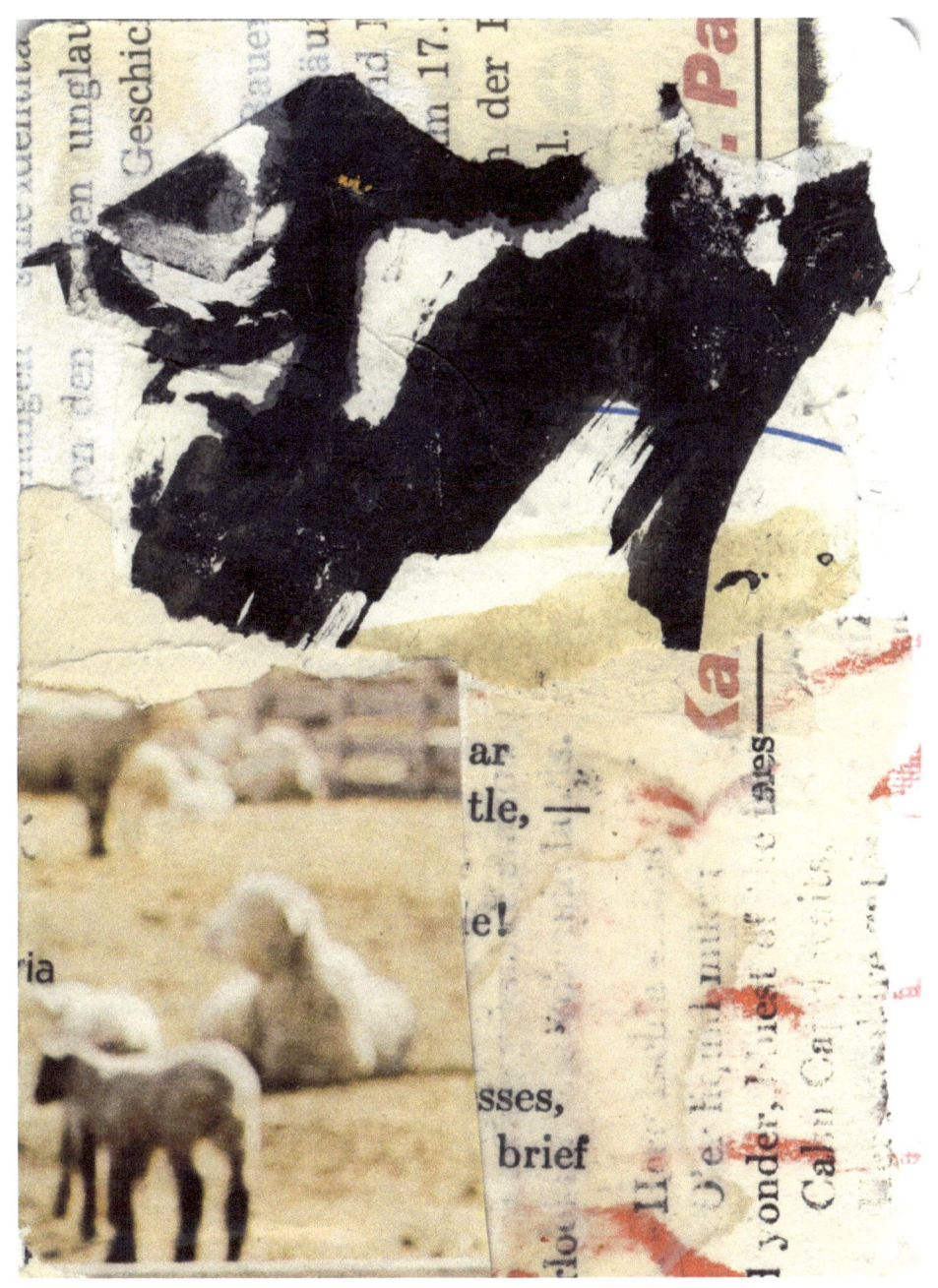

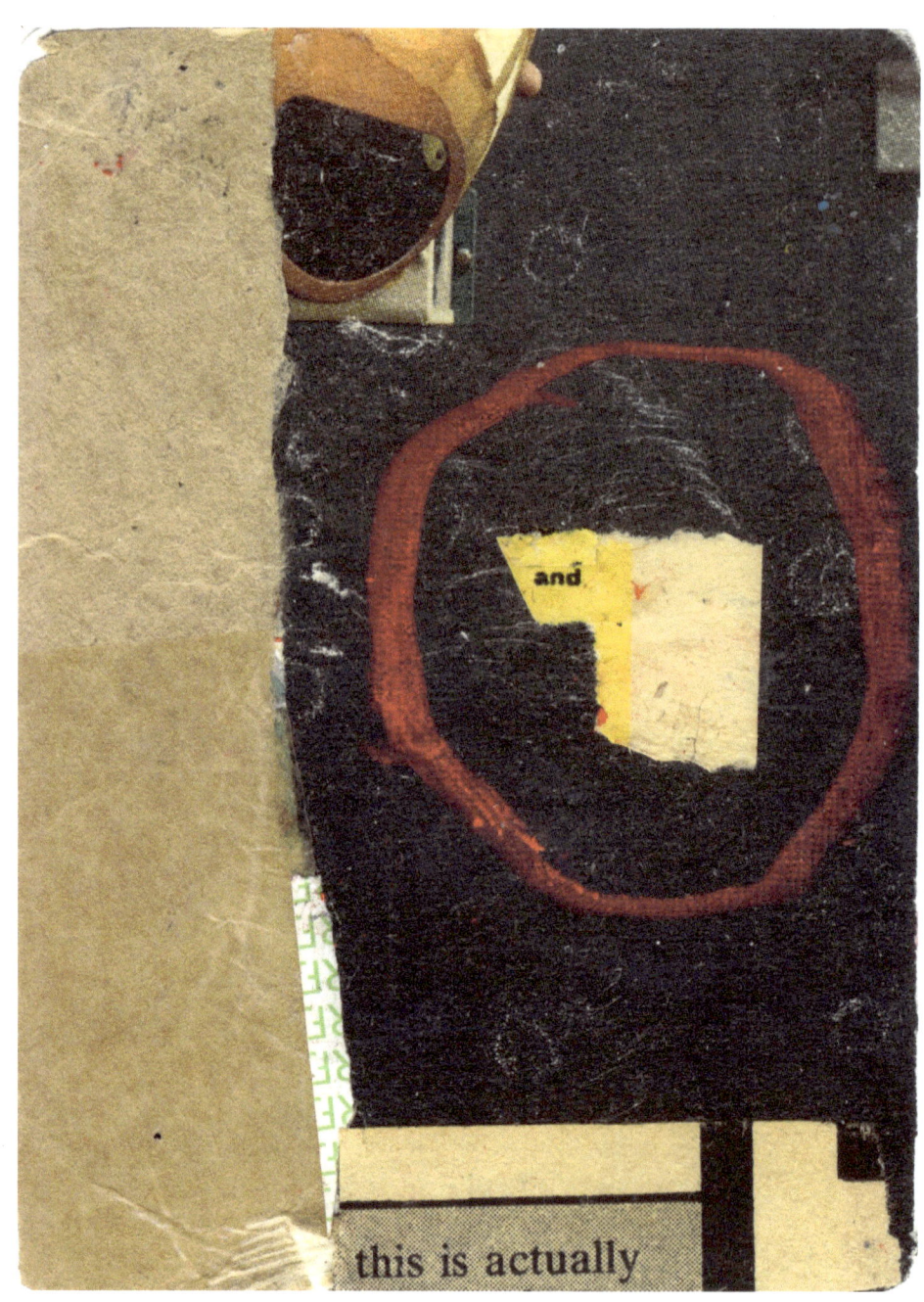

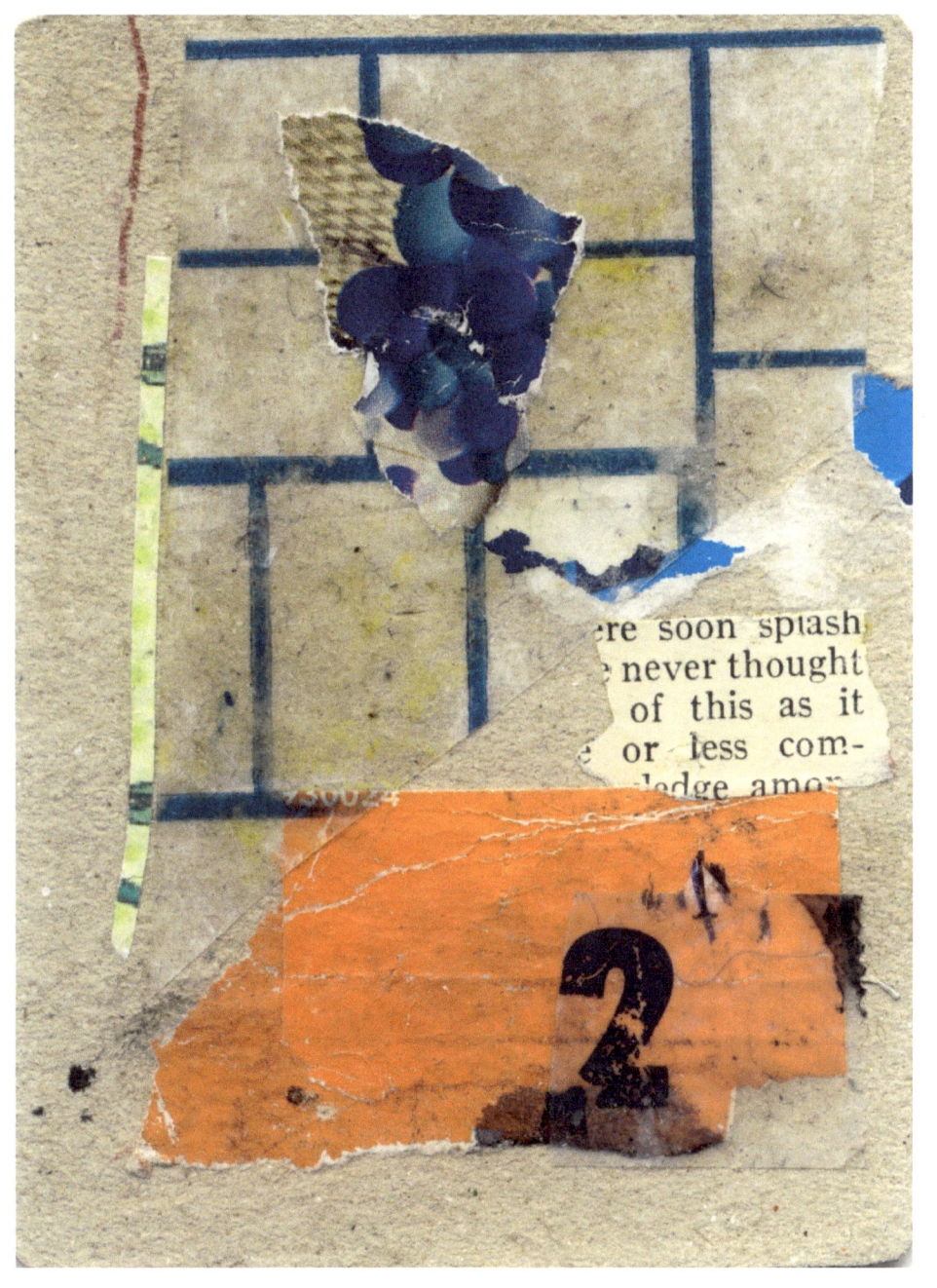

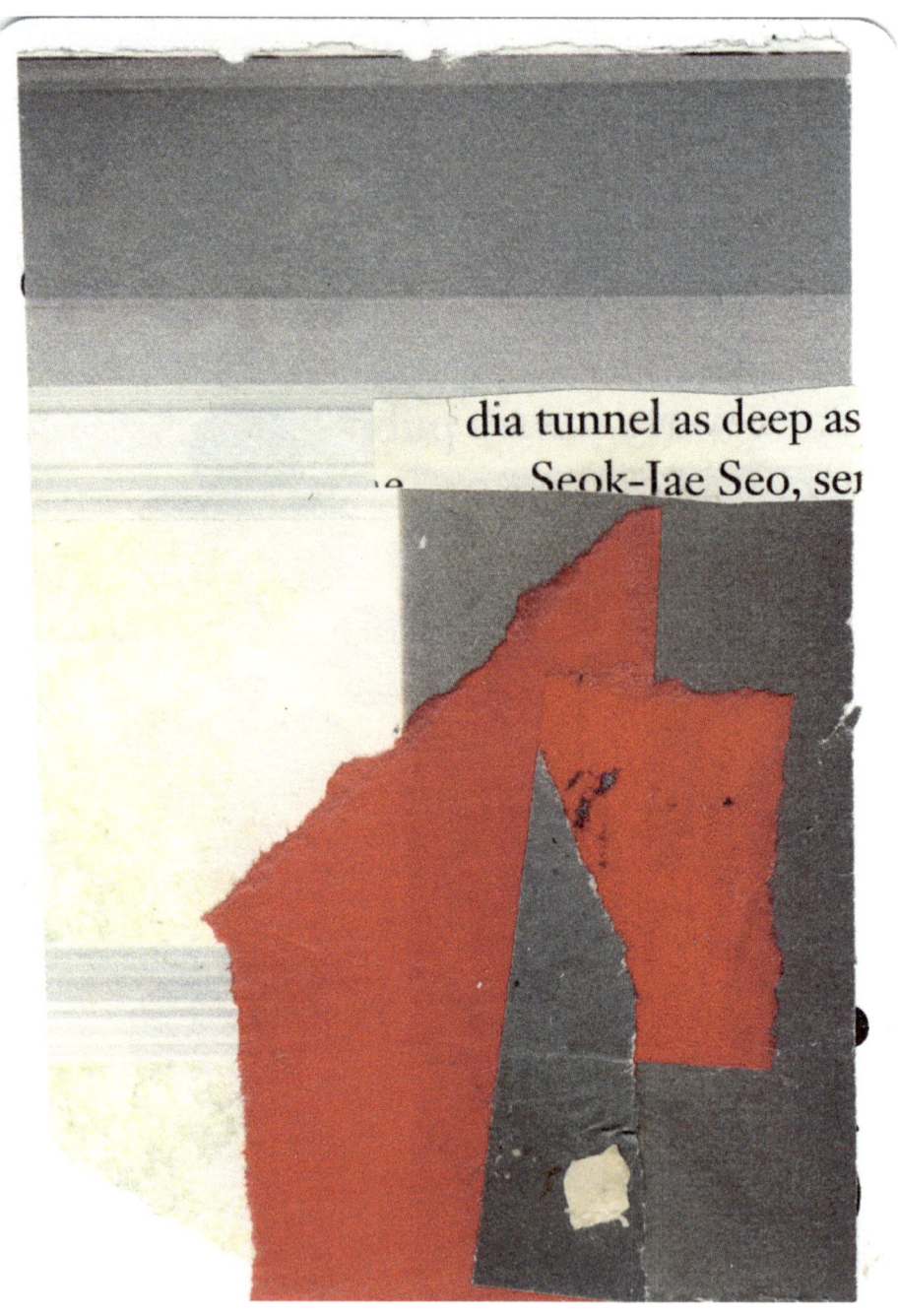

dia tunnel as deep as

Seok-Jae Seo, se

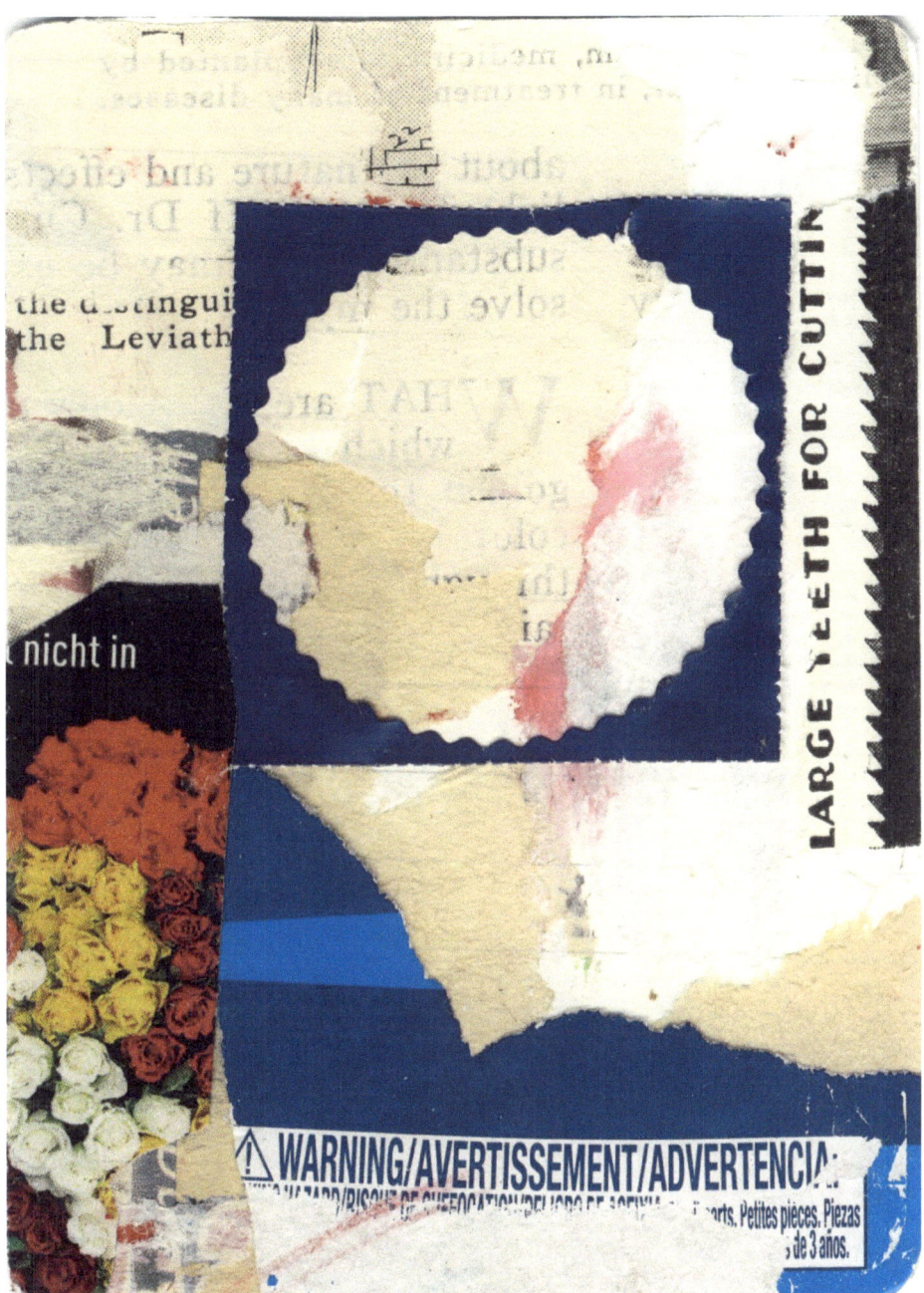

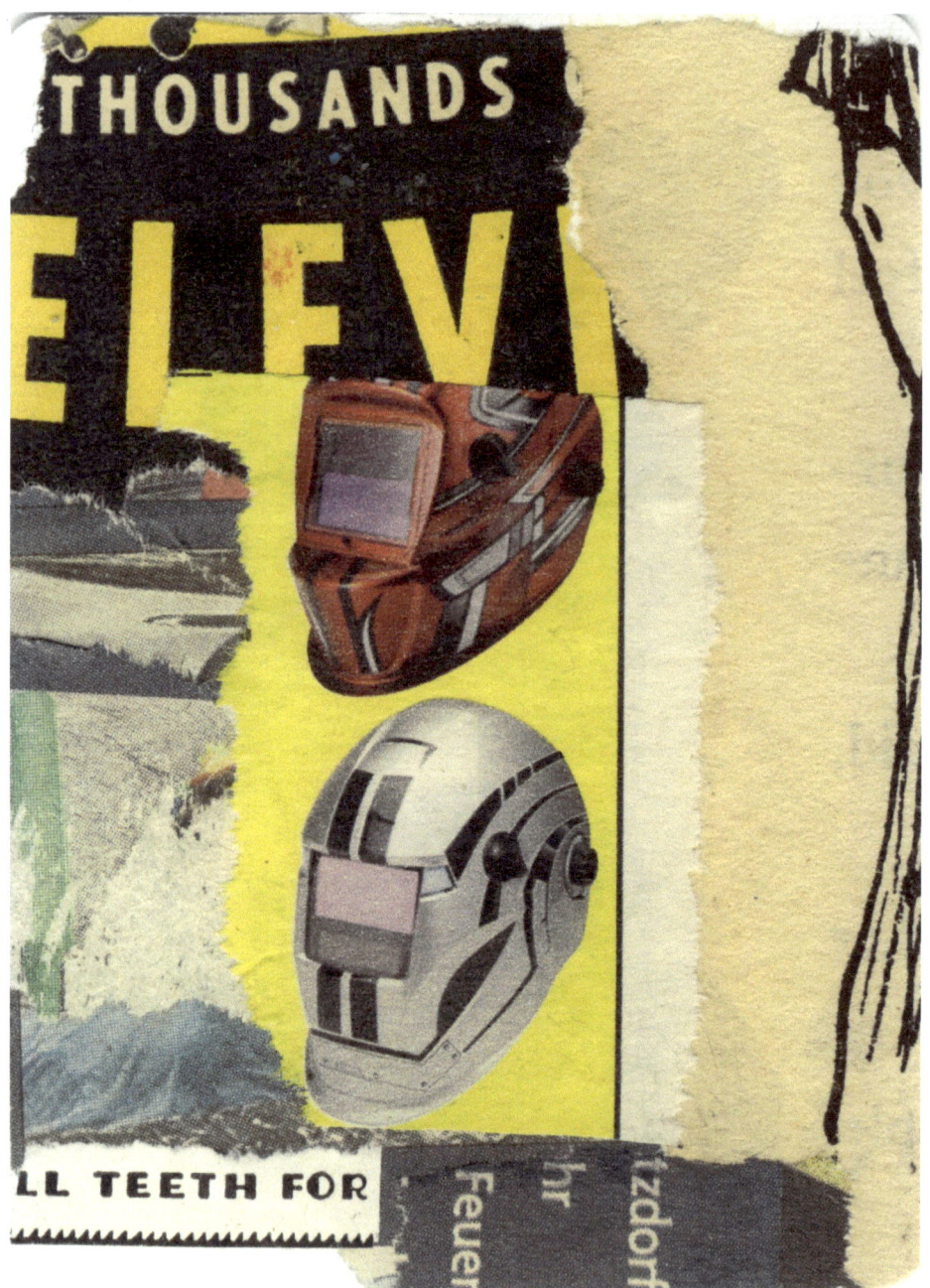

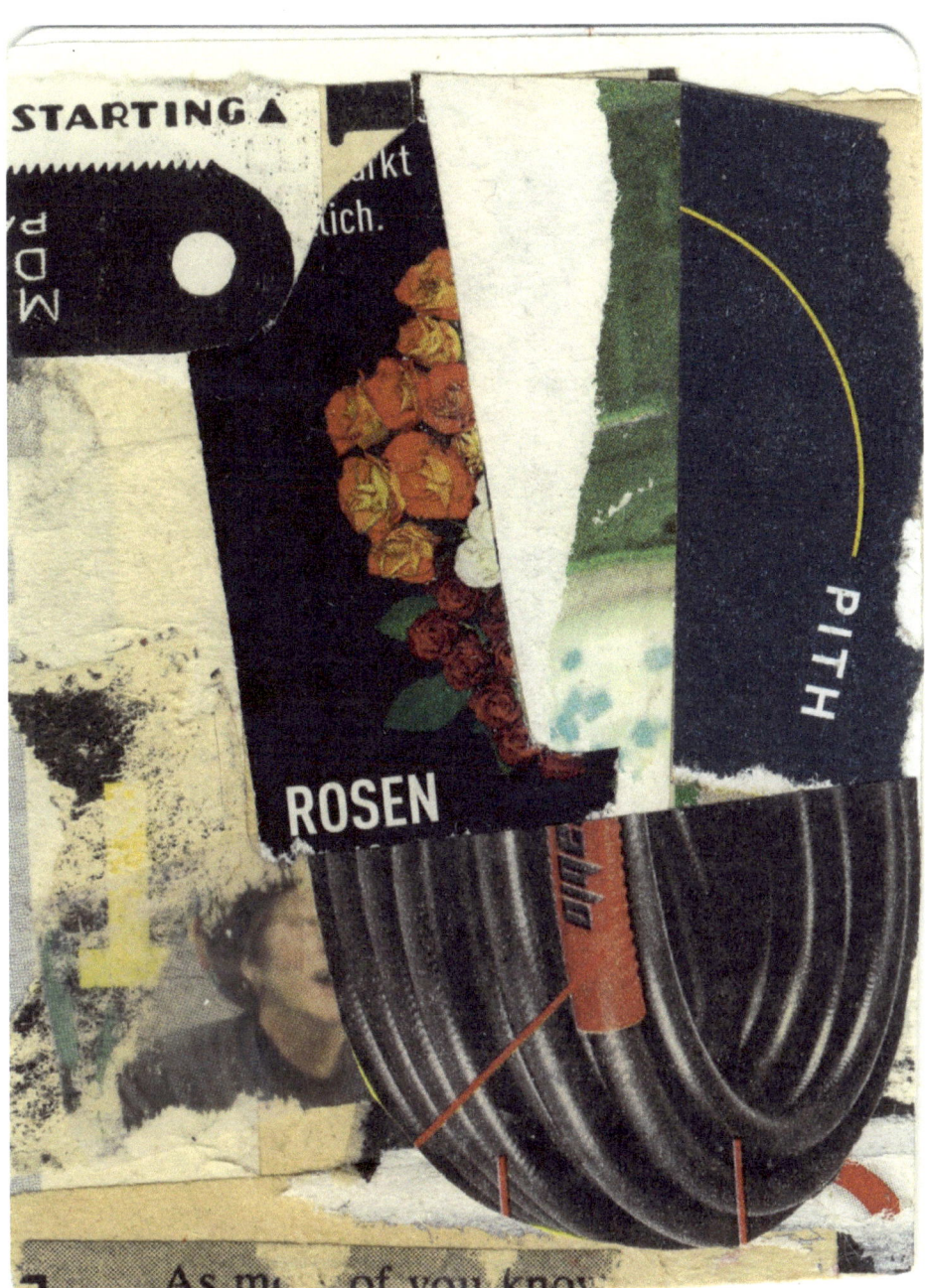

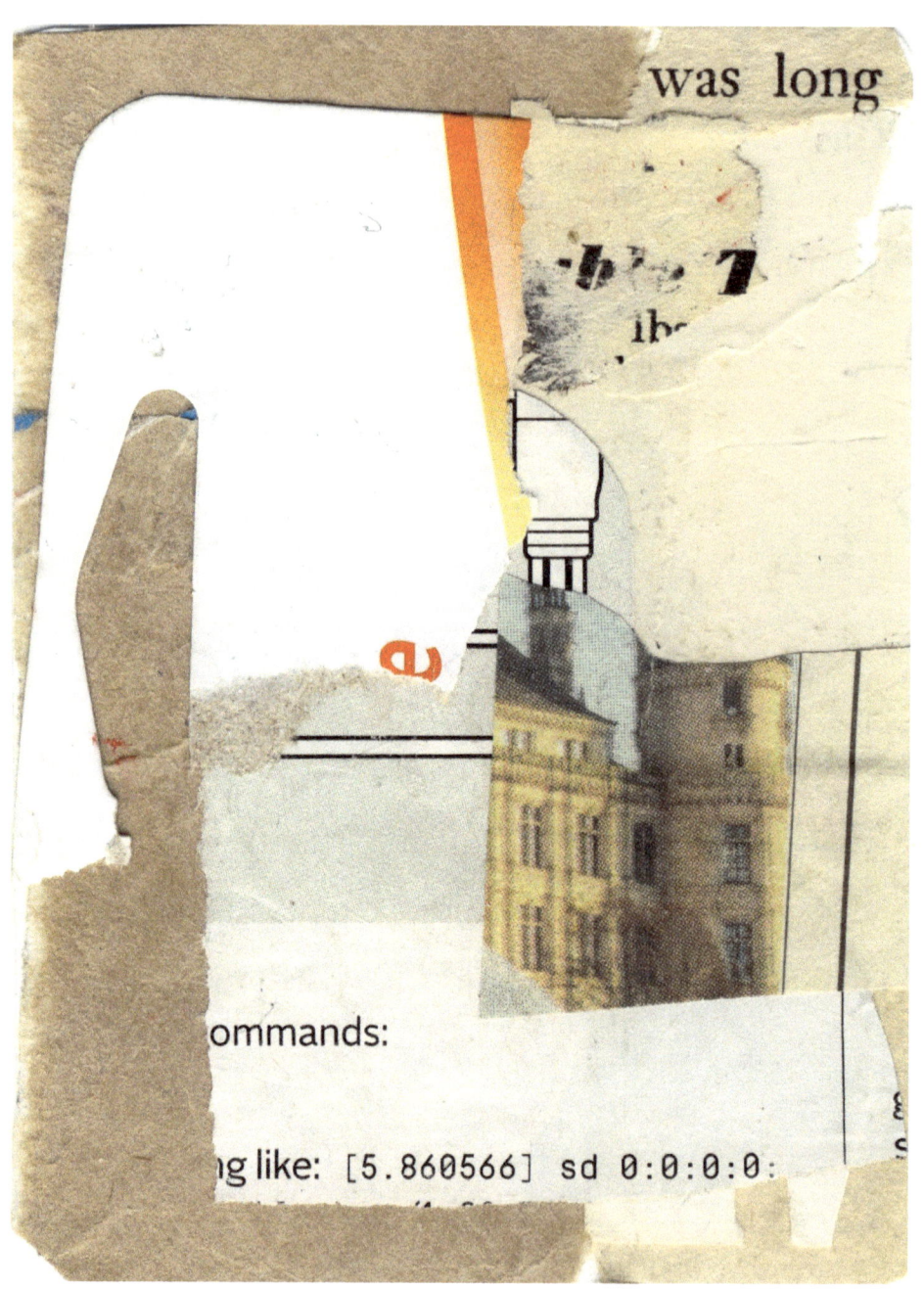

was long

ommands:

g like: [5.860566] sd 0:0:0:0:

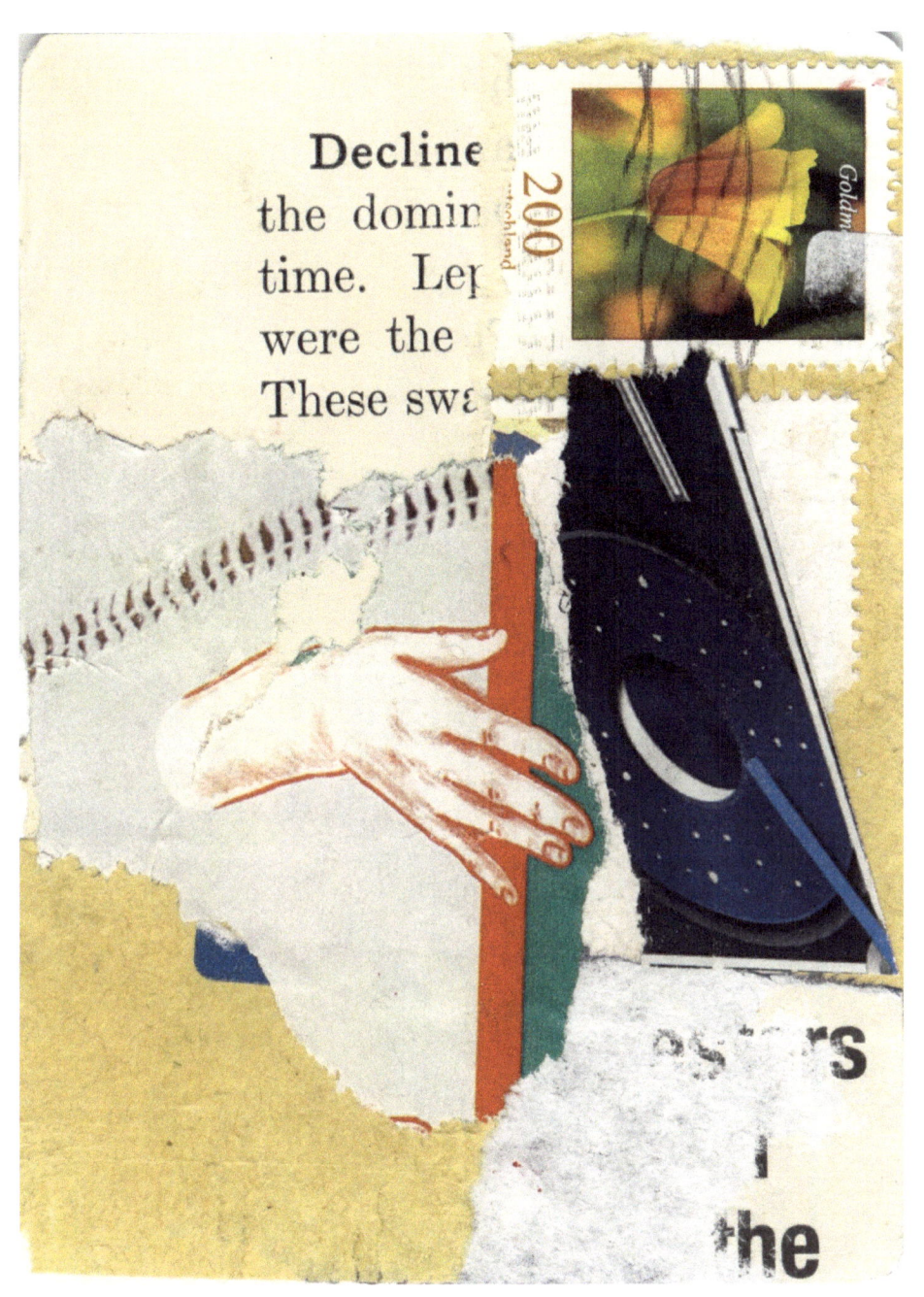

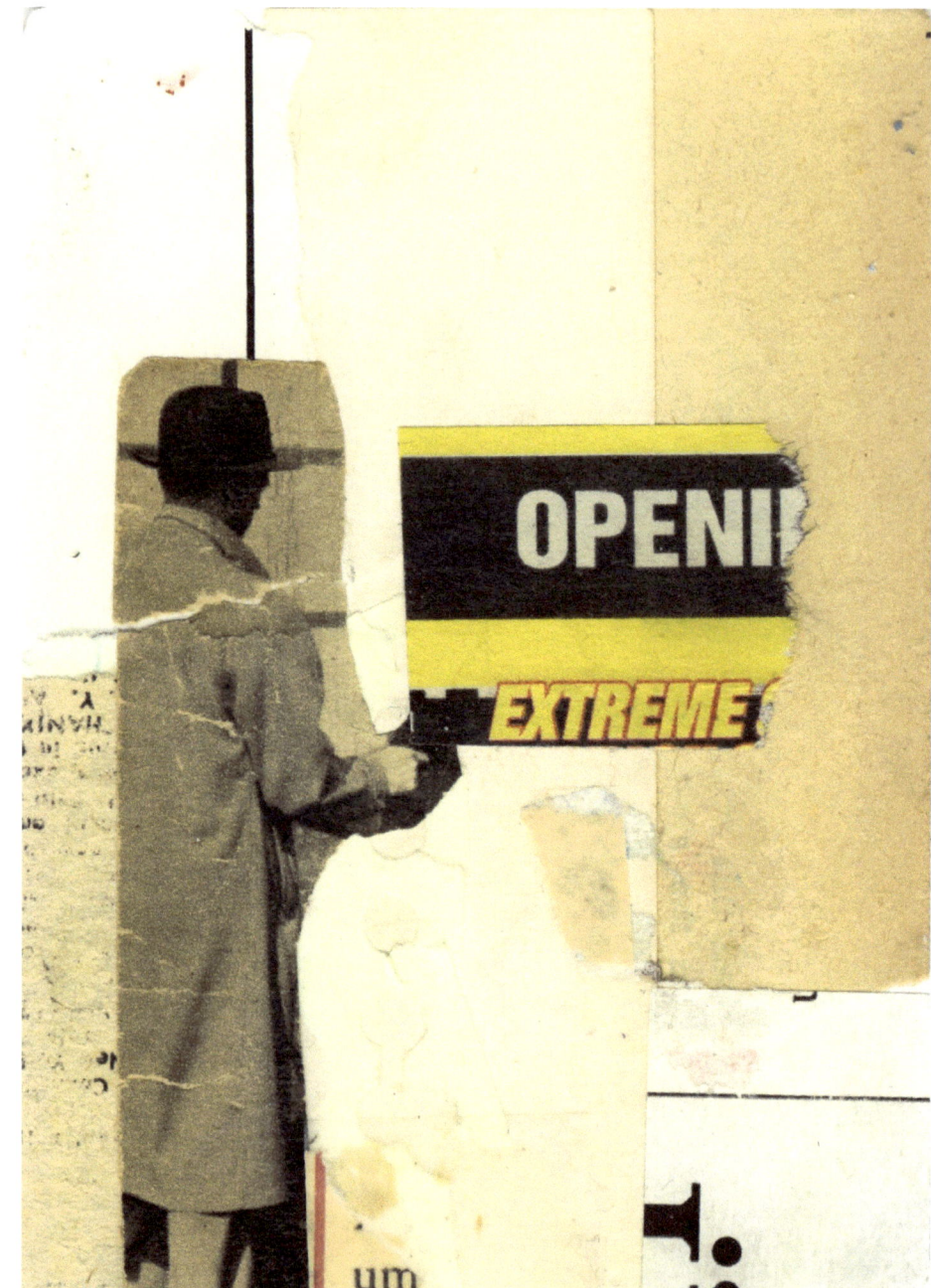

We don't have to
tune out the ch

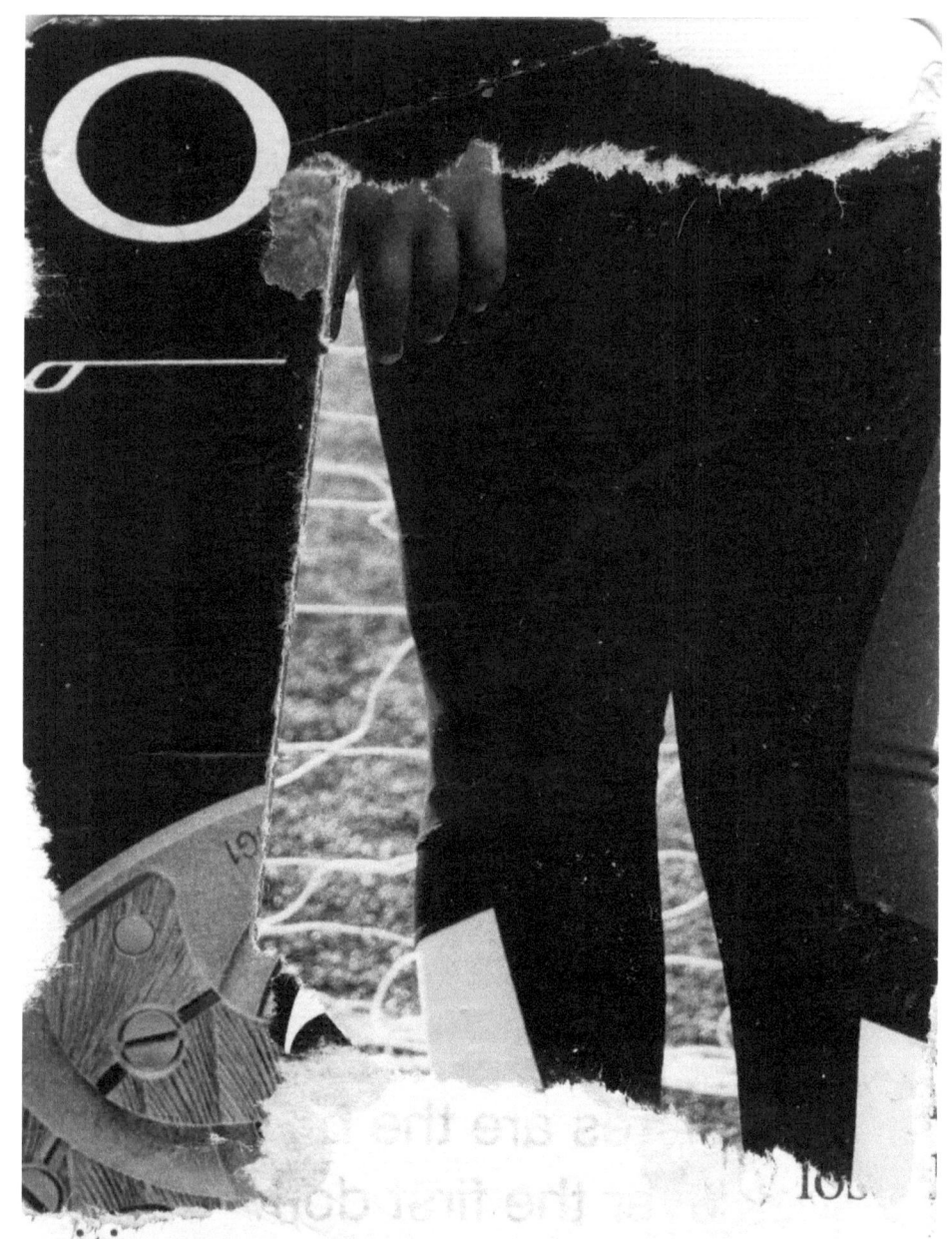

citizens could topple governments.

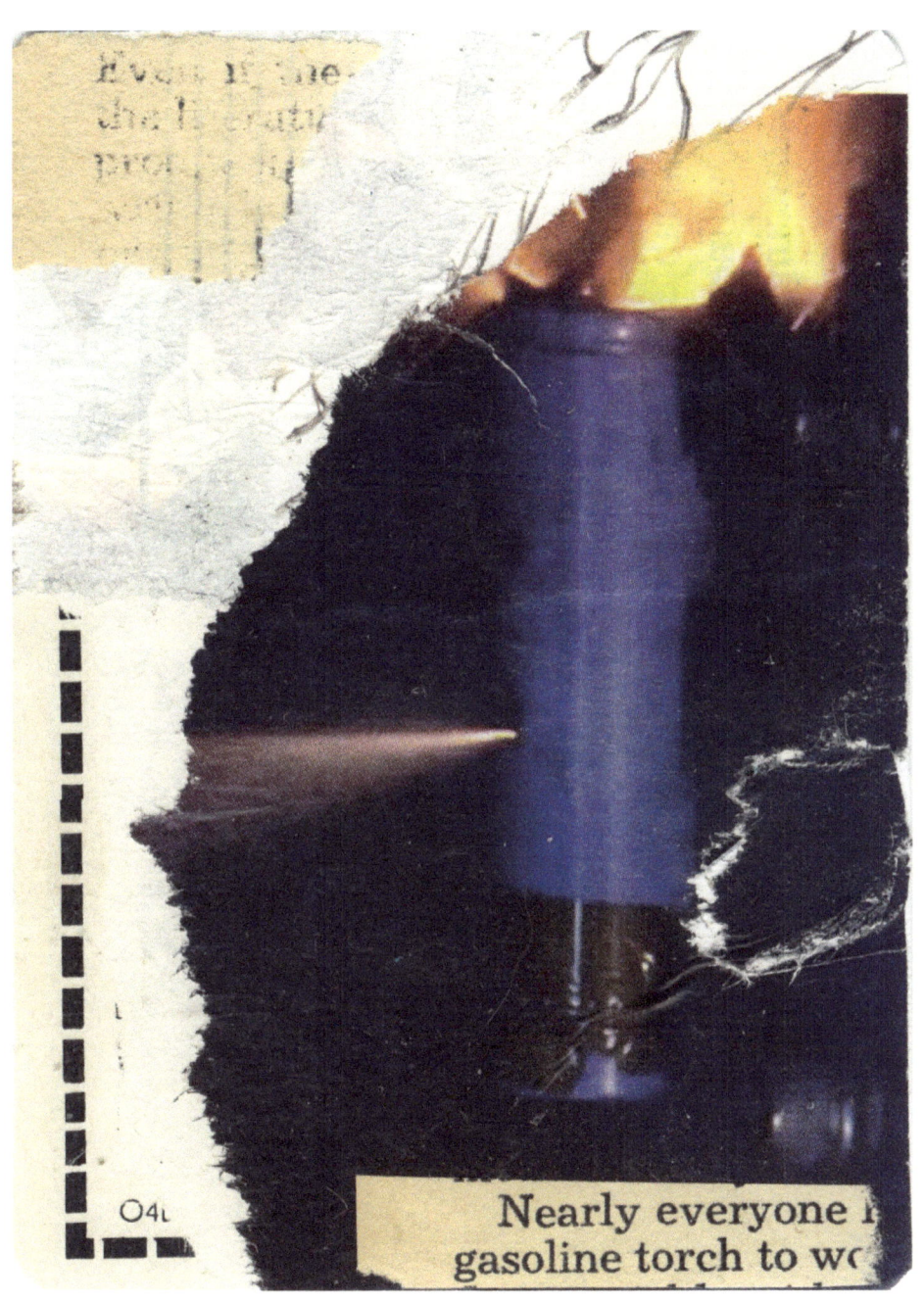

Even if the
the literature
produce the
sur

O4

Nearly everyone
gasoline torch to wo

HOME

I am nearer [...]
    Than I ever have been before;

Aber ein Idealist sind Sie schon, od[...]

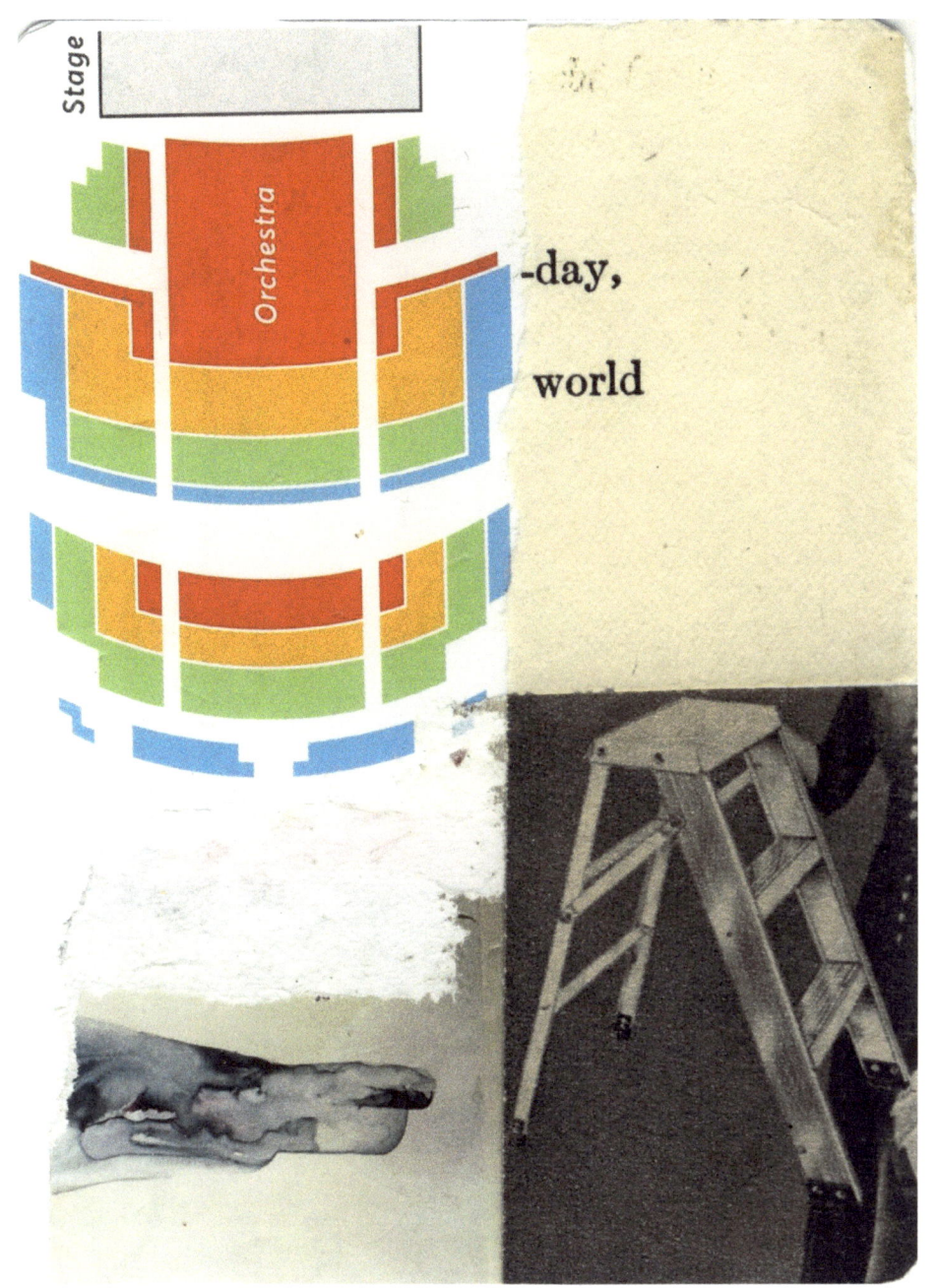

-day,

world

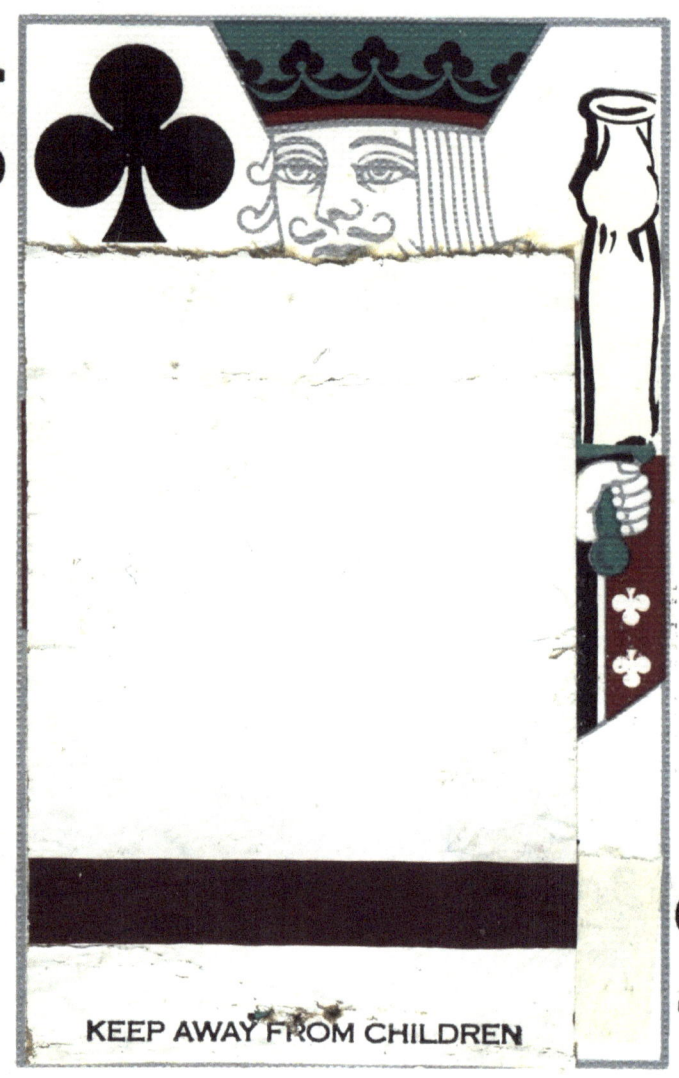

KEEP AWAY FROM CHILDREN

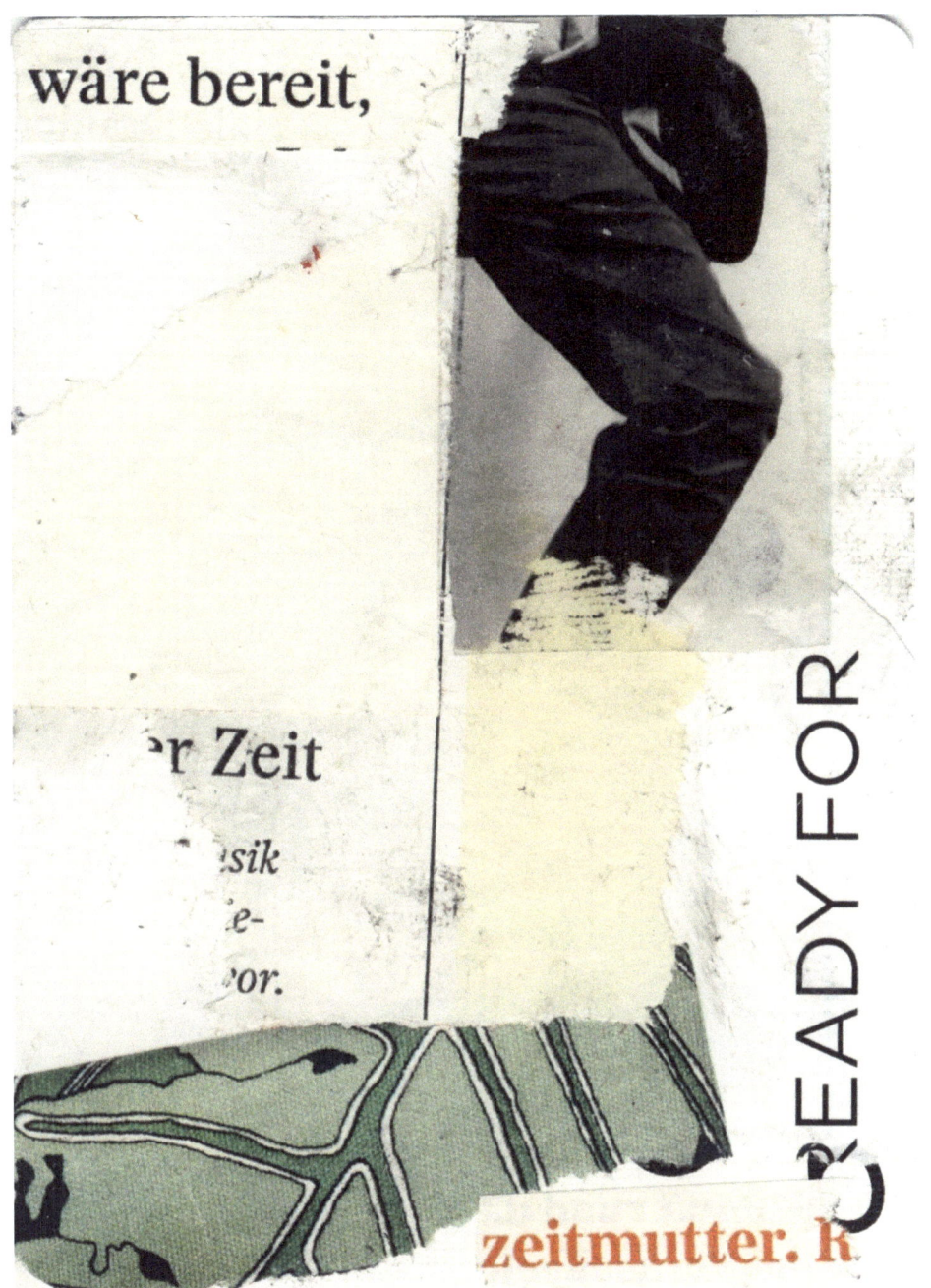

wäre bereit,

r Zeit

sik
e-
or.

READY FOR

zeitmutter. R

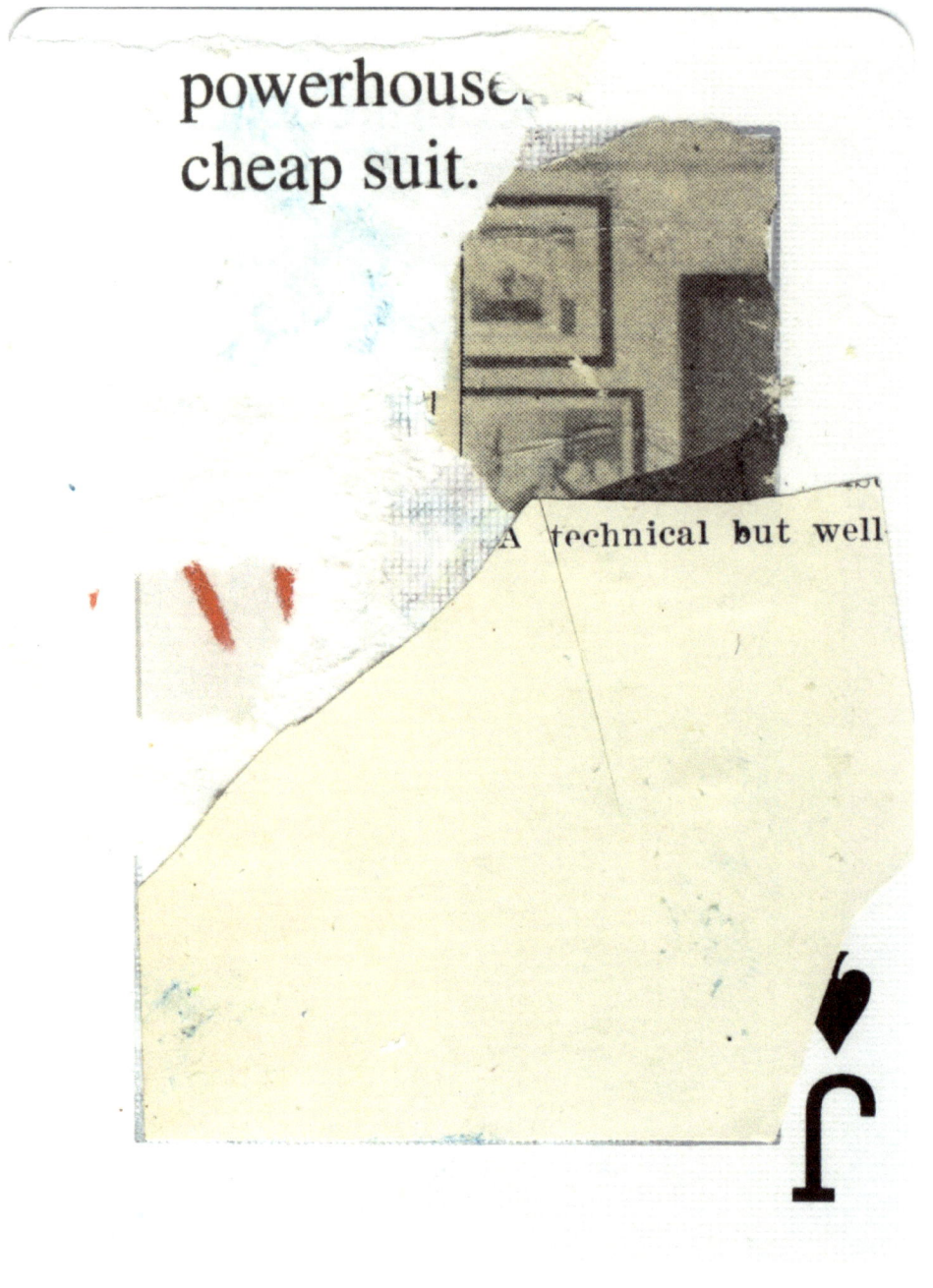

powerhouse

cheap suit.

A technical but well

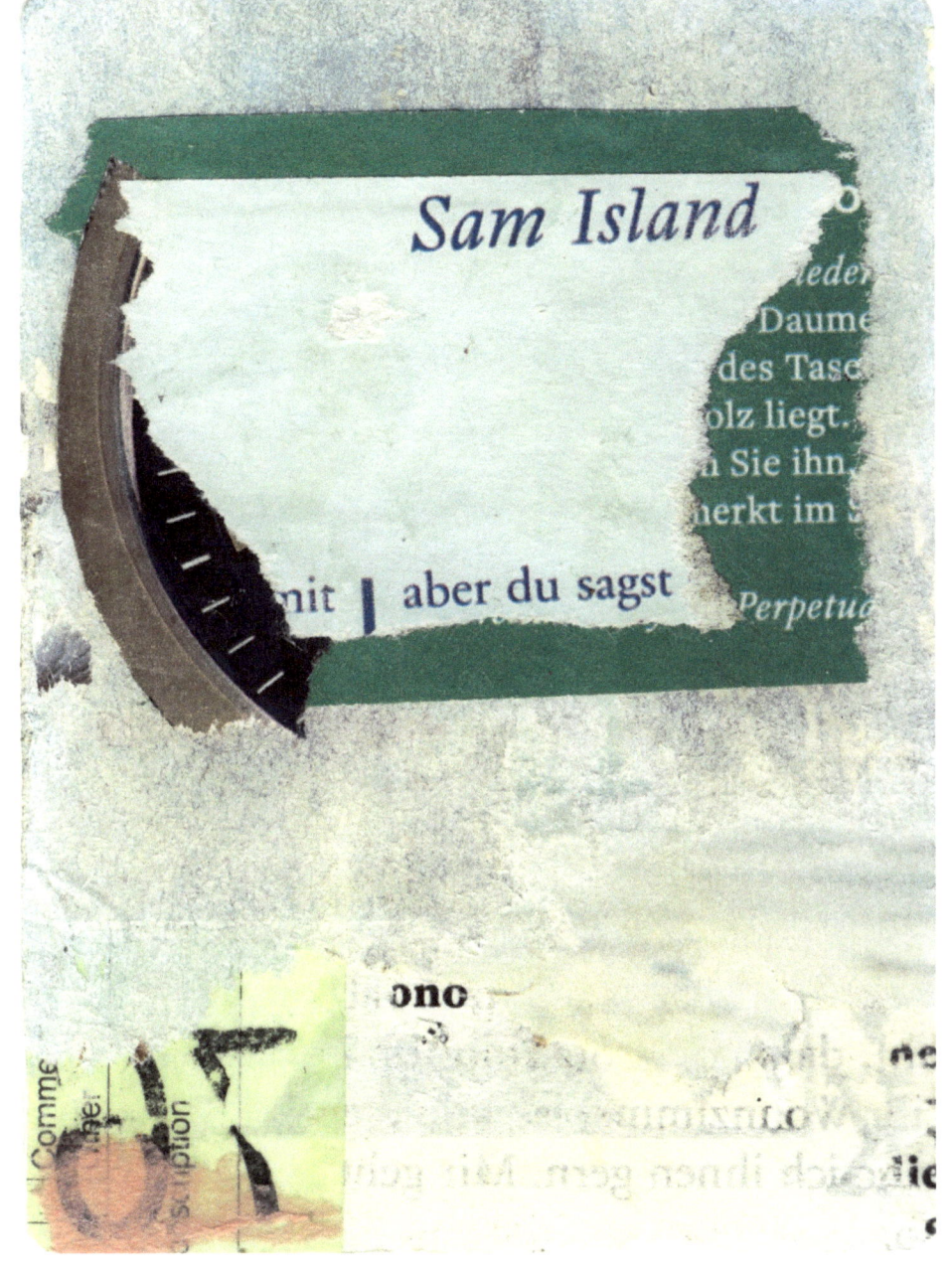

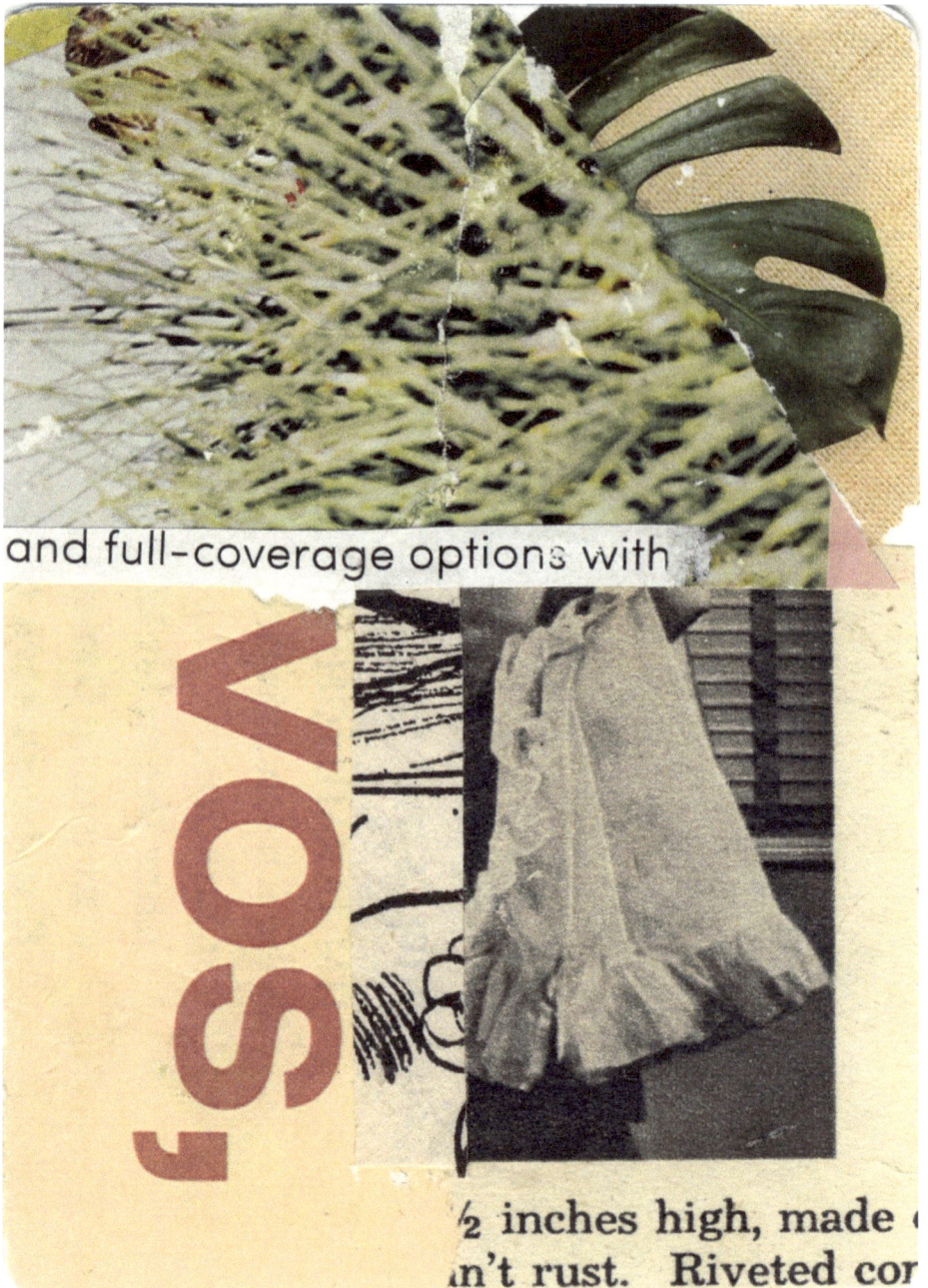

and full-coverage options with

VOS'

½ inches high, made
n't rust. Riveted cor

free of the stone.
s.

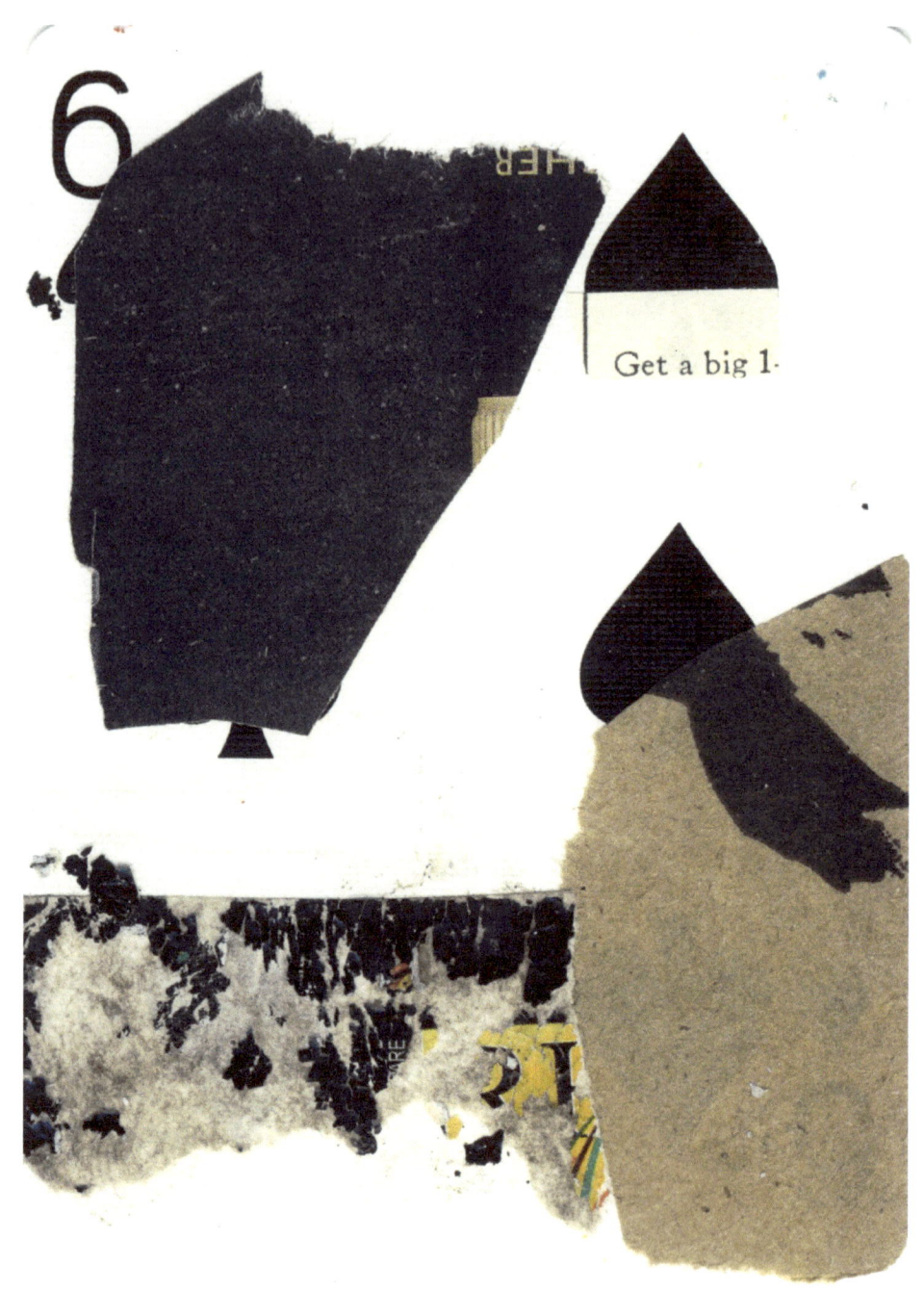

10 ♠

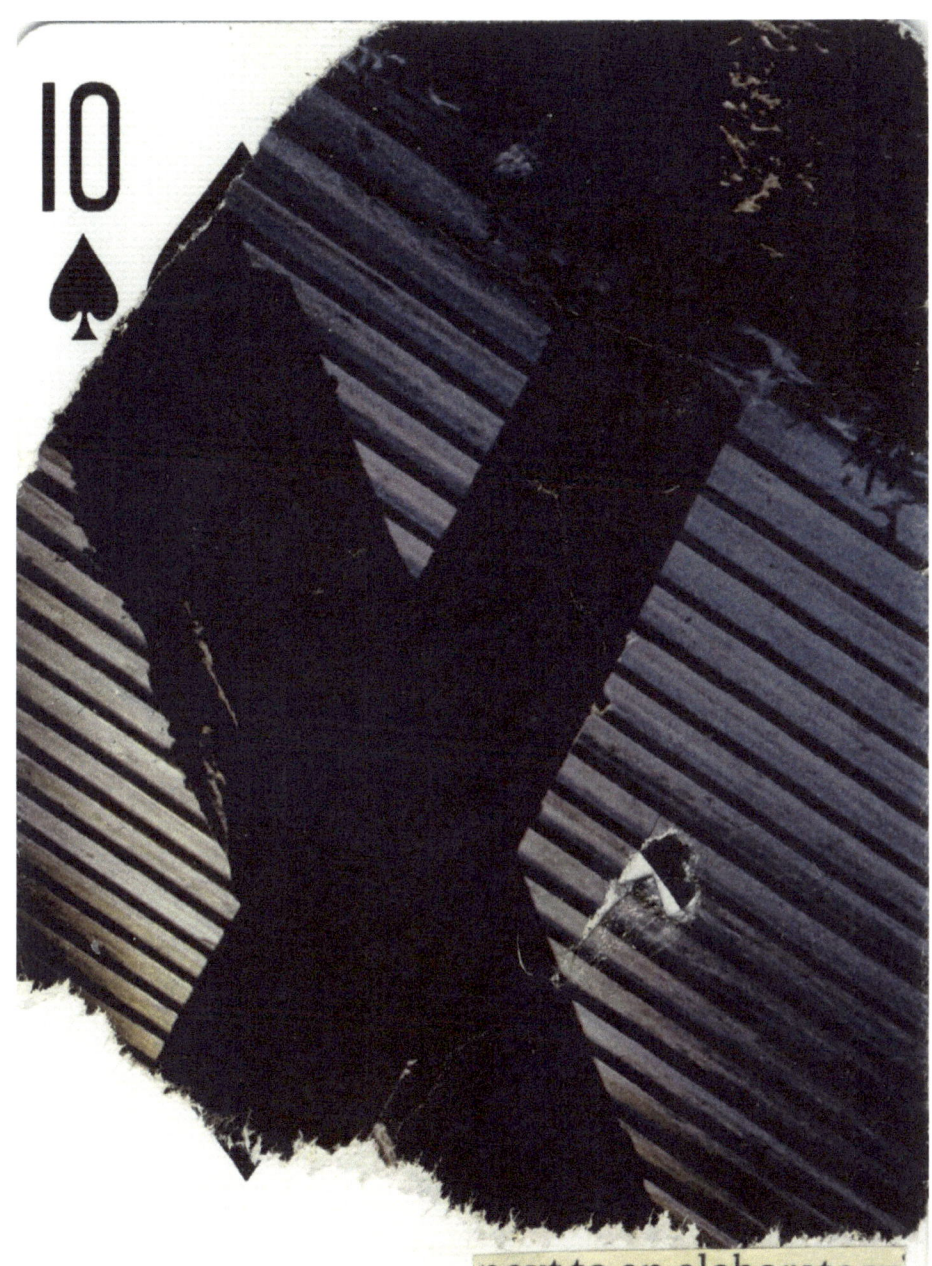

next to an elaborate w

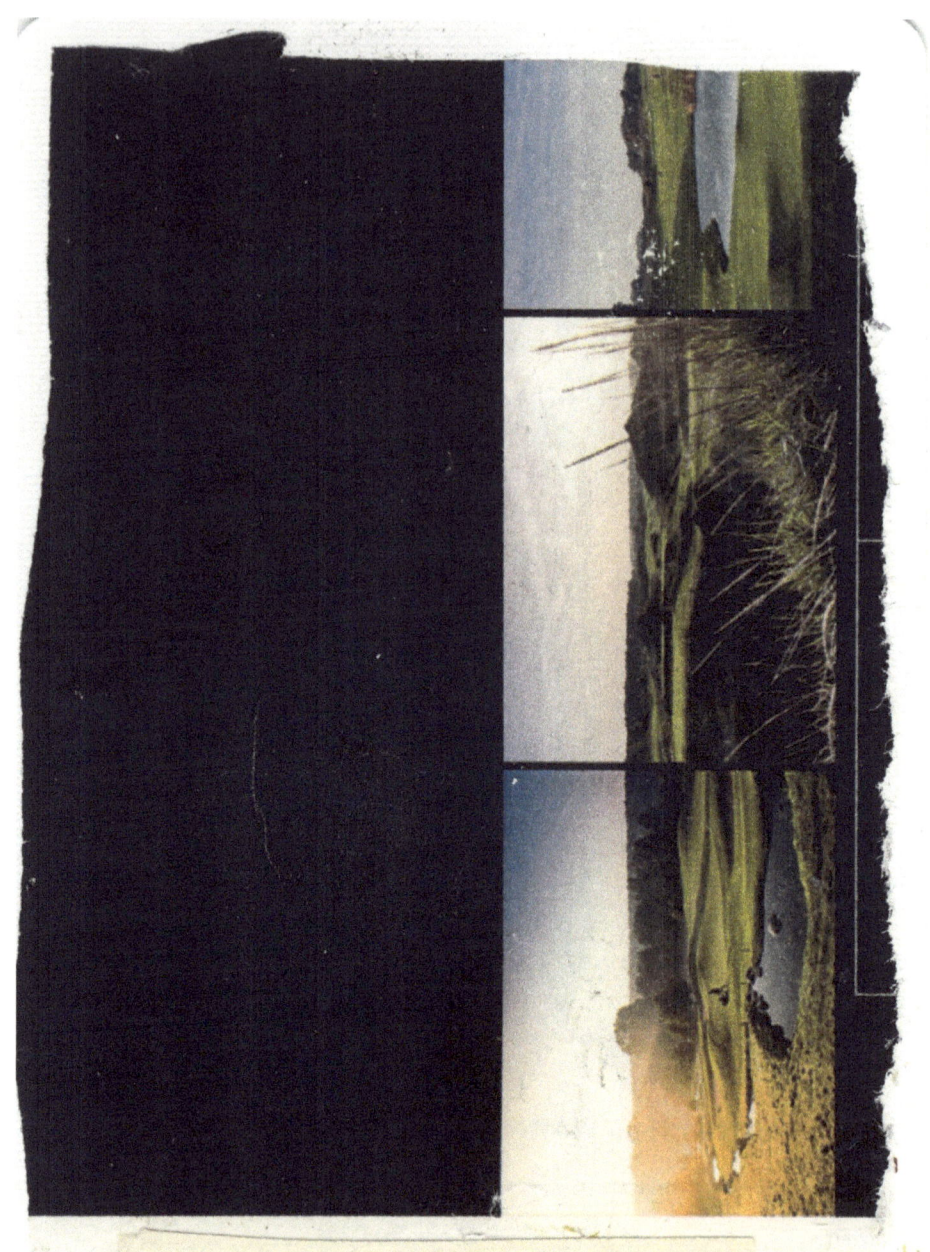

$$a^5 = a \times a \times a \times a \times a$$

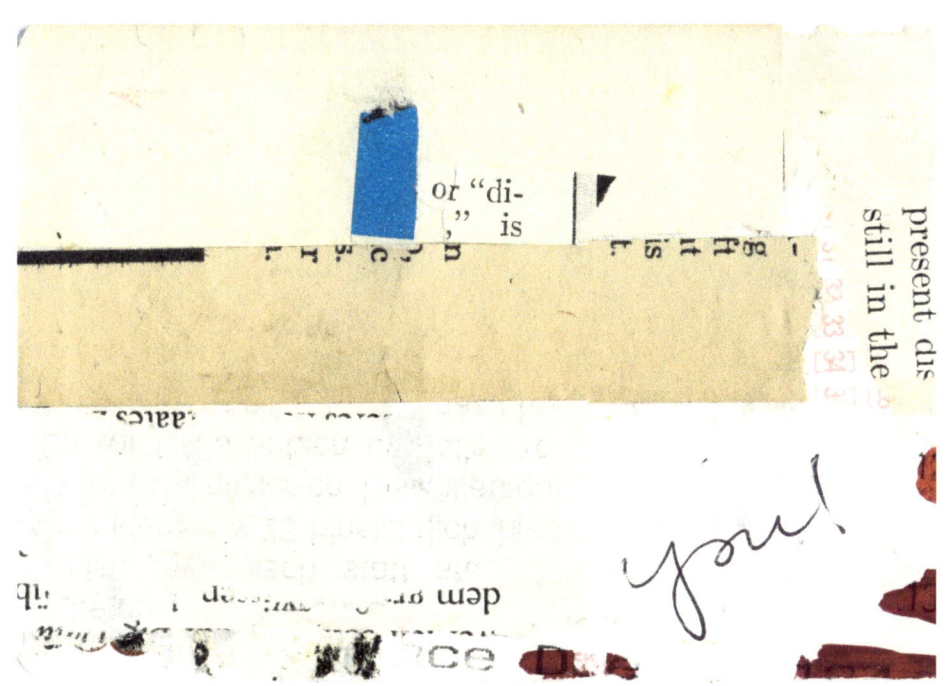

or "di-
," is

present as
still in the

you!

are singing round my window.......

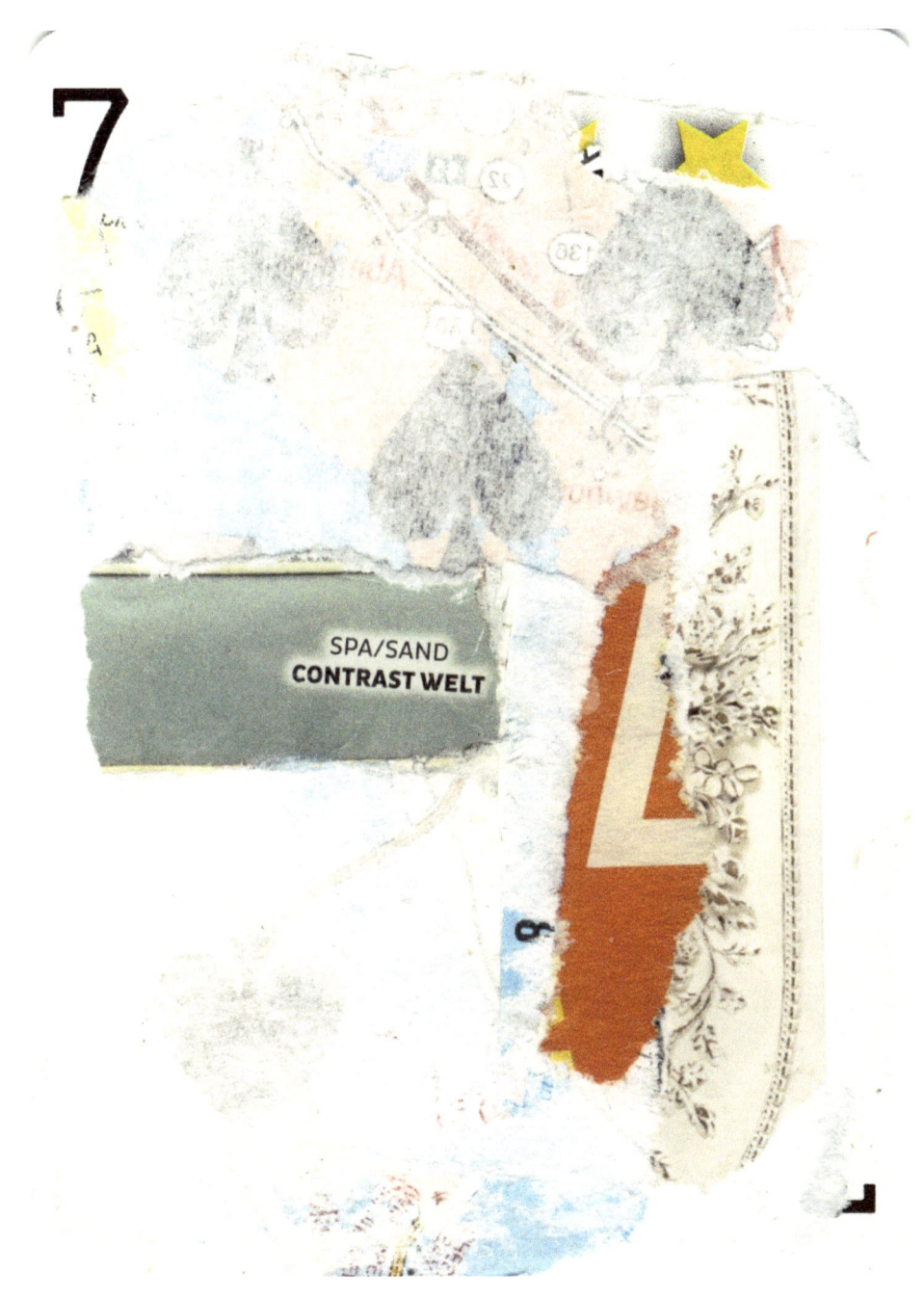

SPA/SAND
CONTRAST WELT

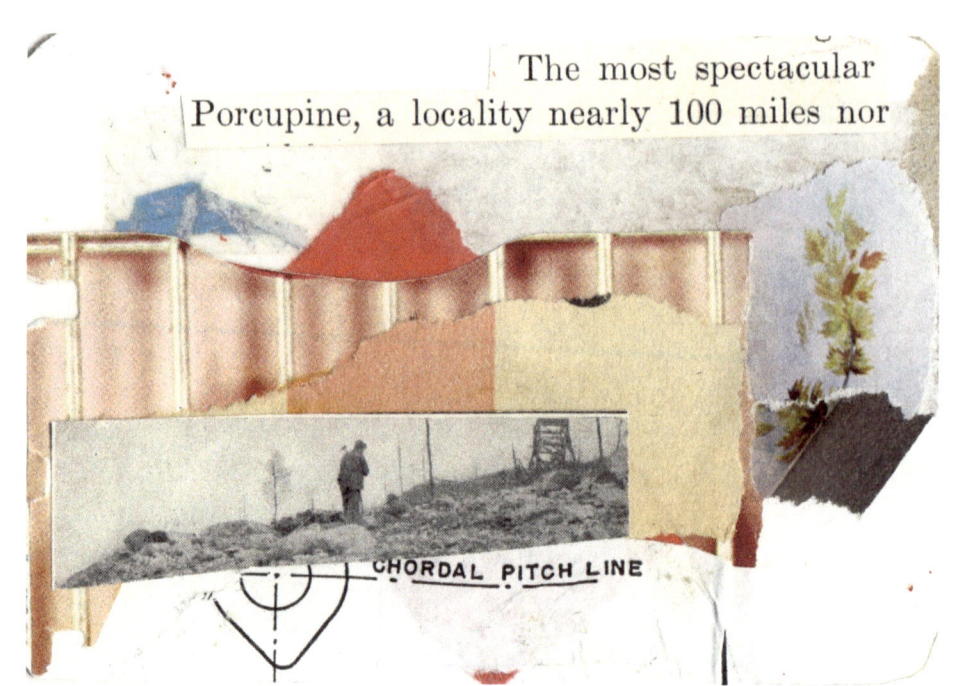

The most spectacular
Porcupine, a locality nearly 100 miles nor

CHORDAL PITCH LINE

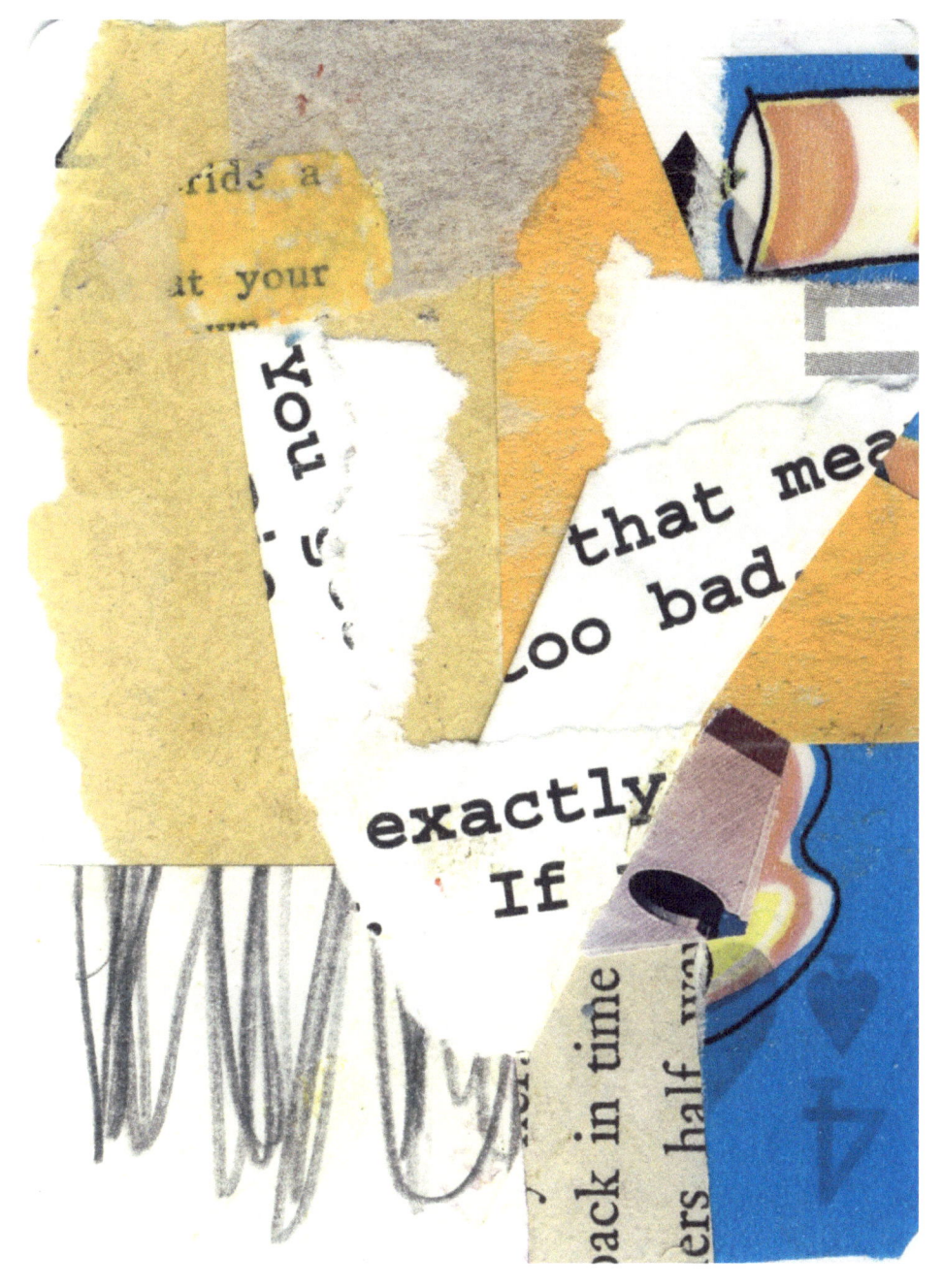

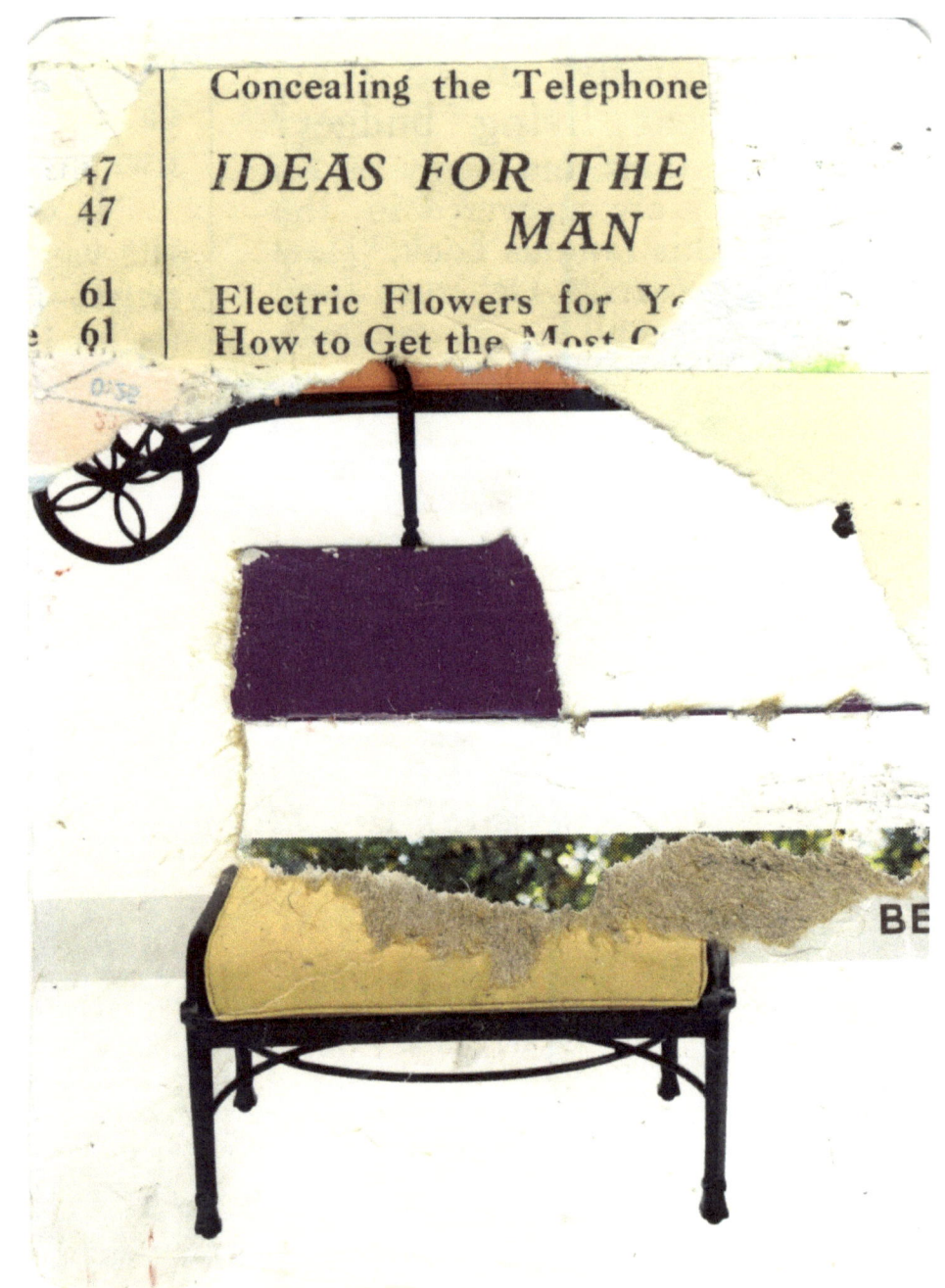

Concealing the Telephone

IDEAS FOR THE MAN

47
47

61   Electric Flowers for Y
61   How to Get the Most C

BE

www.ingramcontent.com/pod-product-compliance
Lightning Source LLC
Chambersburg PA
CBHW041301180526
45172CB00003B/921